INNER REFLECTIONS

ENGAGEMENT CALENDAR 2017

SELECTIONS FROM THE WRITINGS OF
PARAMAHANSA YOGANANDA

SELF-REALIZATION FELLOWSHIP

FRONT COVER:
Lily of the Valley plant with dewdrops
Photograph by Don Paulson
Design by Shawn Freeman

NOTE: *Holidays and other observed dates are included for the United States (U.S.), Canada, United Kingdom (U.K.), Australia, and New Zealand (N.Z.).*
Moon phases, equinoxes, and solstices are based on Pacific Standard Time (UTC – 8 hours).

Self-Realization Fellowship, 3880 San Rafael Avenue, Los Angeles, California 90065-3219, U.S.A.

Printed in Italy
4835-J3739

The scenery of mountains painted on the ever-changing azure canvas of the sky,
the mysterious mechanism of the human body, the rose, the green grass carpet,
the magnanimity of souls, the loftiness of minds,
the depth of love — all these things remind us
of a God who is beautiful and noble.

—Paramahansa Yogananda

THE PHOTOGRAPHS IN THIS CALENDAR are accompanied by selections from the writings of Paramahansa Yogananda, whose timeless and universal teachings have awakened many, of all races, cultures, and creeds, to a deeper awareness of the one reality that sustains and unites us all.

Whether spread over the vast heavens or hidden in the exquisite delicacy of a tiny flower, nature's beauty is always beckoning, inviting us to look behind the outward form and sense the presence of God within.

We hope that the thoughts and images in these pages will bring you inspiration and encouragement in the days and weeks of the coming year.

Lily of the Valley plant with dewdrops   Photograph by Don Paulson

This is my New Year's wish for you: that you all reach the land beyond your dreams, where there is peace and joy eternal. May you realize the fulfillment of whatever strong good wish you release in the ether.

—Paramahansa Yogananda

Lake Antorno and Dolomite Mountains, South Tyrol, Italy   Photograph by Tom Mackie

December/January

26
monday

Boxing Day (Canada, U.K., Australia, N.Z.)

27
tuesday

28
wednesday

New Moon ●

29
thursday

30
friday

31
saturday

1
sunday

New Year's Day

DECEMBER 2016

S	M	T	W	T	F	S
				1	2	3
4	5	6	7	8	9	10
11	12	13	14	15	16	17
18	19	20	21	22	23	24
25	26	27	28	29	30	31

JANUARY

S	M	T	W	T	F	S
1	2	3	4	5	6	7
8	9	10	11	12	13	14
15	16	17	18	19	20	21
22	23	24	25	26	27	28
29	30	31				

January

2
monday

New Year's Day (Observed)

3
tuesday

4
wednesday

5
thursday

Paramahansa Yogananda's Birthday First Quarter ◐

6
friday

7
saturday

8
sunday

JANUARY

S	M	T	W	T	F	S
1	2	3	4	5	6	7
8	9	10	11	12	13	14
15	16	17	18	19	20	21
22	23	24	25	26	27	28
29	30	31				

FEBRUARY

S	M	T	W	T	F	S
			1	2	3	4
5	6	7	8	9	10	11
12	13	14	15	16	17	18
19	20	21	22	23	24	25
26	27	28				

God has given inner strength for the tree to survive the harshest winters.
You are no less endowed.
The wintertimes of life come not to destroy you,
but to stimulate you to fresh enthusiasm and constructive effort.

—Paramahansa Yogananda

Red barn in snow   Photograph by Bernard Friel

Our little minds are part of the omnipotent mind of God.
Beneath the wave of our consciousness is the infinite ocean of His consciousness.

—Paramahansa Yogananda

Choppy seas off Oahu, Hawaii   Photograph by Stephen Kirkpatrick

January

9
monday

10
tuesday

11
wednesday

12
thursday

Full Moon ○

13
friday

14
saturday

15
sunday

JANUARY

S	M	T	W	T	F	S
1	2	3	4	5	6	7
8	9	10	11	12	13	14
15	16	17	18	19	20	21
22	23	24	25	26	27	28
29	30	31				

FEBRUARY

S	M	T	W	T	F	S
			1	2	3	4
5	6	7	8	9	10	11
12	13	14	15	16	17	18
19	20	21	22	23	24	25
26	27	28				

January

16
monday

Martin Luther King, Jr.'s Birthday (Observed)

17
tuesday

18
wednesday

19
thursday

Last Quarter ◑

20
friday

21
saturday

22
sunday

JANUARY

S	M	T	W	T	F	S
1	2	3	4	5	6	7
8	9	10	11	12	13	14
15	16	17	18	19	20	21
22	23	24	25	26	27	28
29	30	31				

FEBRUARY

S	M	T	W	T	F	S
			1	2	3	4
5	6	7	8	9	10	11
12	13	14	15	16	17	18
19	20	21	22	23	24	25
26	27	28				

Introspection is a mirror in which to see recesses of your mind that otherwise would remain hidden from you....Analyze what you are, what you wish to become, and what shortcomings are impeding you.... Endeavor to make yourself what you should be and what you want to be.

—Paramahansa Yogananda

Flamingo   Photograph by Claudio Contreras

You cannot buy peace; you must know how to manufacture it within,
in the stillness of your daily practices in meditation.
When you think that you have reached the utmost depth of silence and calmness,
go deeper still. In the silence you will receive from God the answers to your life's problems.

—Paramahansa Yogananda

Sunrise, Moraine Lake, Banff National Park, Canada   Photograph by Dennis Frates

January

23
monday

24
tuesday

25
wednesday

26
thursday

Australia Day (Australia)

27
friday

New Moon ●

28
saturday

29
sunday

JANUARY

S	M	T	W	T	F	S
1	2	3	4	5	6	7
8	9	10	11	12	13	14
15	16	17	18	19	20	21
22	23	24	25	26	27	28
29	30	31				

FEBRUARY

S	M	T	W	T	F	S
			1	2	3	4
5	6	7	8	9	10	11
12	13	14	15	16	17	18
19	20	21	22	23	24	25
26	27	28				

January/February

30
monday

31
tuesday

1
wednesday

2
thursday

3
friday

First Quarter ◐

4
saturday

5
sunday

JANUARY

S	M	T	W	T	F	S
1	2	3	4	5	6	7
8	9	10	11	12	13	14
15	16	17	18	19	20	21
22	23	24	25	26	27	28
29	30	31				

FEBRUARY

S	M	T	W	T	F	S
			1	2	3	4
5	6	7	8	9	10	11
12	13	14	15	16	17	18
19	20	21	22	23	24	25
26	27	28				

Go out of your way to make others happy. You cannot please everybody, but to those souls who cross your path, give kindness and love.

—Paramahansa Yogananda

Playful squirrel   Photograph by Jim Nelson/500PX

O Spirit Beautiful, open the window of nature and the windows of our minds, that we may behold Thee in all Thy glory.

—Paramahansa Yogananda

Cathedral Rock, Sedona, Arizona   Photograph by Marion Owen

February

6
monday

7
tuesday

8
wednesday

9
thursday

Full Moon ◯

10
friday

February

S	M	T	W	T	F	S
			1	2	3	4
5	6	7	8	9	10	11
12	13	14	15	16	17	18
19	20	21	22	23	24	25
26	27	28				

March

S	M	T	W	T	F	S
			1	2	3	4
5	6	7	8	9	10	11
12	13	14	15	16	17	18
19	20	21	22	23	24	25
26	27	28	29	30	31	

11
saturday

12
sunday

February

13
monday

14
tuesday
St. Valentine's Day

15
wednesday

16
thursday

17
friday

18
saturday
Last Quarter ◑

19
sunday

February

S	M	T	W	T	F	S
			1	2	3	4
5	6	7	8	9	10	11
12	13	14	15	16	17	18
19	20	21	22	23	24	25
26	27	28				

March

S	M	T	W	T	F	S
			1	2	3	4
5	6	7	8	9	10	11
12	13	14	15	16	17	18
19	20	21	22	23	24	25
26	27	28	29	30	31	

Droplets of love sparkle in true souls,
but in Spirit alone is found the sea of love.

—Paramahansa Yogananda

Dewdrops on flower petal Photograph by Juliana Nan/500PX

Every morning when you begin your day, think not only of serving your own welfare, but of how many others you can help.

—Paramahansa Yogananda

Black-tailed deer, Olympic National Park, Washington Photograph by Michael Wheatley

February

Presidents' Day

20 monday

21 tuesday

22 wednesday

23 thursday

24 friday

February

S	M	T	W	T	F	S
			1	2	3	4
5	6	7	8	9	10	11
12	13	14	15	16	17	18
19	20	21	22	23	24	25
26	27	28				

March

S	M	T	W	T	F	S
			1	2	3	4
5	6	7	8	9	10	11
12	13	14	15	16	17	18
19	20	21	22	23	24	25
26	27	28	29	30	31	

25 saturday

New Moon ●

26 sunday

February/March

27
monday

28
tuesday

1
wednesday

2
thursday

3
friday

4
saturday

5
sunday

First Quarter ◐

February

S	M	T	W	T	F	S
			1	2	3	4
5	6	7	8	9	10	11
12	13	14	15	16	17	18
19	20	21	22	23	24	25
26	27	28				

March

S	M	T	W	T	F	S
			1	2	3	4
5	6	7	8	9	10	11
12	13	14	15	16	17	18
19	20	21	22	23	24	25
26	27	28	29	30	31	

I stand on the rocky strand of matter and look longingly for
Thy distant shores of etheric beauty. I have summoned divine inner architects
that are building across the gulf a rainbow bridge of my constant remembrance of Thee.

—Paramahansa Yogananda

Peschanaya Bay, Lake Baikal, Siberia, Russia Photograph by Per-Andre Hoffman/AGE Fotostock

Live simply and take life more easily. Happiness lies in giving yourself time to think and to introspect. Be alone once in a while, and remain more in silence.

—Paramahansa Yogananda

Indian Peafowl, Yala National Park, Sri Lanka   Photograph by Kevin Schafer/Minden Pictures

March

6
monday

7
tuesday

Paramahansa Yogananda's Mahasamadhi

8
wednesday

9
thursday

Sri Yukteswar's Mahasamadhi

10
friday

11
saturday

12
sunday

Daylight Saving Time begins (U.S. and Canada)   Full Moon ○

March

S	M	T	W	T	F	S
			1	2	3	4
5	6	7	8	9	10	11
12	13	14	15	16	17	18
19	20	21	22	23	24	25
26	27	28	29	30	31	

April

S	M	T	W	T	F	S
						1
2	3	4	5	6	7	8
9	10	11	12	13	14	15
16	17	18	19	20	21	22
23/30	24	25	26	27	28	29

March

13
monday

14
tuesday

15
wednesday

16
thursday

17
friday

St. Patrick's Day

18
saturday

19
sunday

MARCH

S	M	T	W	T	F	S
			1	2	3	4
5	6	7	8	9	10	11
12	13	14	15	16	17	18
19	20	21	22	23	24	25
26	27	28	29	30	31	

APRIL

S	M	T	W	T	F	S
						1
2	3	4	5	6	7	8
9	10	11	12	13	14	15
16	17	18	19	20	21	22
23/30	24	25	26	27	28	29

See Him in the glorious colors in the dawn and sunset....
It is His invisible hand that is painting scenery on the sky.

—Paramahansa Yogananda

Great Sand Dunes National Park, Colorado   Photograph by George H. H. Huey

Let me drink forever from the sourceless river of Thine inexhaustibility.

—Paramahansa Yogananda

Elowah Falls, Columbia River Gorge, Oregon   Photograph by Dave Welling

March

20
monday

Vernal Equinox Last Quarter ◑

21
tuesday

22
wednesday

23
thursday

24
friday

MARCH

S	M	T	W	T	F	S
			1	2	3	4
5	6	7	8	9	10	11
12	13	14	15	16	17	18
19	20	21	22	23	24	25
26	27	28	29	30	31	

APRIL

S	M	T	W	T	F	S
						1
2	3	4	5	6	7	8
9	10	11	12	13	14	15
16	17	18	19	20	21	22
23/30	24	25	26	27	28	29

25
saturday

26
sunday

Daylight Saving Time begins (European Union)

March/April

27
monday

New Moon ●

28
tuesday

29
wednesday

30
thursday

31
friday

1
saturday

2
sunday

March

S	M	T	W	T	F	S
			1	2	3	4
5	6	7	8	9	10	11
12	13	14	15	16	17	18
19	20	21	22	23	24	25
26	27	28	29	30	31	

April

S	M	T	W	T	F	S
						1
2	3	4	5	6	7	8
9	10	11	12	13	14	15
16	17	18	19	20	21	22
23/30	24	25	26	27	28	29

O Spirit, teach me to find the fountain of infinite power within myself, that I may drink of its soothing waters and quench the thirst of all my needs.

—Paramahansa Yogananda

Eurasian blue tit drinking   Photograph by A. Jeffry/500PX

Let us learn to build inner mansions of wisdom in the unfading garden of peace that blooms with the million-hued blossoms of beautiful soul qualities.

—Paramahansa Yogananda

Avalanche lilies, Mt. Rainier National Park, Washington   Photograph by Kathy Mahan

April

3
monday

First Quarter ◐

4
tuesday

5
wednesday

6
thursday

7
friday

April

S	M	T	W	T	F	S
						1
2	3	4	5	6	7	8
9	10	11	12	13	14	15
16	17	18	19	20	21	22
23/30	24	25	26	27	28	29

May

S	M	T	W	T	F	S
	1	2	3	4	5	6
7	8	9	10	11	12	13
14	15	16	17	18	19	20
21	22	23	24	25	26	27
28	29	30	31			

8
saturday

9
sunday

April

10 monday

Passover begins Full Moon ○

11 tuesday

12 wednesday

13 thursday

14 friday

Good Friday

15 saturday

16 sunday

Easter Sunday

April

S	M	T	W	T	F	S
						1
2	3	4	5	6	7	8
9	10	11	12	13	14	15
16	17	18	19	20	21	22
23/30	24	25	26	27	28	29

May

S	M	T	W	T	F	S
	1	2	3	4	5	6
7	8	9	10	11	12	13
14	15	16	17	18	19	20
21	22	23	24	25	26	27
28	29	30	31			

The blossoms of life in the garden of earthly existence are enchanting to behold. But somewhere there is a fount of Beauty and Intelligence, even more enthralling, from which we have come and into which we shall merge again.

—Paramahansa Yogananda

Columbine flowers, Crested Butte, Colorado   Photograph by Thomas Kraft

Through meditation one can experience a stable,
silent inner peace that can be a permanently soothing background
for all harmonious or trialsome activities demanded by life's responsibilities.

—Paramahansa Yogananda

Knuthojdsmossen Wetland, Vastmanland, Sweden Photograph by Roine Magnusson/First Light

April

17
monday

Easter Monday (All except U.S. & Scotland)

18
tuesday

19
wednesday

Last Quarter ◑

20
thursday

21
friday

APRIL

S	M	T	W	T	F	S
						1
2	3	4	5	6	7	8
9	10	11	12	13	14	15
16	17	18	19	20	21	22
23/30	24	25	26	27	28	29

MAY

S	M	T	W	T	F	S
	1	2	3	4	5	6
7	8	9	10	11	12	13
14	15	16	17	18	19	20
21	22	23	24	25	26	27
28	29	30	31			

22
saturday

Earth Day

23
sunday

April

24
monday

25
tuesday

26
wednesday

New Moon ●

27
thursday

28
friday

29
saturday

30
sunday

April

S	M	T	W	T	F	S
						1
2	3	4	5	6	7	8
9	10	11	12	13	14	15
16	17	18	19	20	21	22
23/30	24	25	26	27	28	29

May

S	M	T	W	T	F	S
	1	2	3	4	5	6
7	8	9	10	11	12	13
14	15	16	17	18	19	20
21	22	23	24	25	26	27
28	29	30	31			

In the kingdom of your love, include not only all human beings, but also animals, flowers, the flocks of stars pasturing on the long savannahs of the blue — all living creatures.

—Paramahansa Yogananda

Lop-eared baby rabbit, London, England   Photograph by Geoff du Feu/AnimalsAnimals

*With the dawn of divine experience, with the dawn of divine joy,
we behold the glimmer of beautiful thoughts and experiences within our heart.*

—Paramahansa Yogananda

Pink Ipe trees, Pantanal, Western Brazil Photograph by Luiz Claudio Marigo/AnimalsAnimals

May

1
monday

2
tuesday

First Quarter ◐

3
wednesday

4
thursday

National Day of Prayer

5
friday

May

S	M	T	W	T	F	S
	1	2	3	4	5	6
7	8	9	10	11	12	13
14	15	16	17	18	19	20
21	22	23	24	25	26	27
28	29	30	31			

6
saturday

June

S	M	T	W	T	F	S
				1	2	3
4	5	6	7	8	9	10
11	12	13	14	15	16	17
18	19	20	21	22	23	24
25	26	27	28	29	30	

7
sunday

May

8
monday

9
tuesday

10
wednesday

Sri Yukteswar's Birthday   Full Moon ○

11
thursday

12
friday

13
saturday

14
sunday

Mother's Day (U.S., Canada, Australia, N.Z.)

May

S	M	T	W	T	F	S
	1	2	3	4	5	6
7	8	9	10	11	12	13
14	15	16	17	18	19	20
21	22	23	24	25	26	27
28	29	30	31			

June

S	M	T	W	T	F	S
				1	2	3
4	5	6	7	8	9	10
11	12	13	14	15	16	17
18	19	20	21	22	23	24
25	26	27	28	29	30	

The beauty in the world bespeaks the creative motherly instinct of God, and when we look upon all the good in Nature, we experience a feeling of tenderness within us — we can see and feel God as Mother in Nature. There is no greater experience than to feel and know that the Cosmic Mother is with you. Watch for the presence of the Mother, because She will look after you in every way.

—Paramahansa Yogananda

Swans, Portland Japanese Garden, Oregon   Photograph by Cindy Kassab/AKM Images

Be the beauty that is in a flower, and the attractiveness that is in a pure mind. When you are attractive in that way you will always have true friends.

—Paramahansa Yogananda

Pink Cherry and Blue Brunnera blossoms   Photograph by Kathy Mahan

May

15
monday

16
tuesday

17
wednesday

18
thursday

Last Quarter ◑

19
friday

MAY

S	M	T	W	T	F	S
	1	2	3	4	5	6
7	8	9	10	11	12	13
14	15	16	17	18	19	20
21	22	23	24	25	26	27
28	29	30	31			

JUNE

S	M	T	W	T	F	S
				1	2	3
4	5	6	7	8	9	10
11	12	13	14	15	16	17
18	19	20	21	22	23	24
25	26	27	28	29	30	

20
saturday

21
sunday

May

22
monday
Victoria Day (Canada)

23
tuesday

24
wednesday

25
thursday
New Moon ●

26
friday

27
saturday

28
sunday

MAY

S	M	T	W	T	F	S
	1	2	3	4	5	6
7	8	9	10	11	12	13
14	15	16	17	18	19	20
21	22	23	24	25	26	27
28	29	30	31			

JUNE

S	M	T	W	T	F	S
				1	2	3
4	5	6	7	8	9	10
11	12	13	14	15	16	17
18	19	20	21	22	23	24
25	26	27	28	29	30	

When you are calm and at peace within, you love everyone and feel friendly toward all. This is the harmony God intended for His creation.

—Paramahansa Yogananda

Blue butterflies Photograph by Mauro Malone/500PX

So long as we are on stage in the drama of life,
we should play our part to the best of our ability....
We must try to understand the purpose of the drama,
and why we have our particular role in it.

—Paramahansa Yogananda

Black bear pup, Rocky Mountain National Park, Colorado Photograph by George Sanker/AKM Images

May/June

29
monday

Memorial Day

30
tuesday

31
wednesday

1
thursday

First Quarter ◐

2
friday

MAY

S	M	T	W	T	F	S
	1	2	3	4	5	6
7	8	9	10	11	12	13
14	15	16	17	18	19	20
21	22	23	24	25	26	27
28	29	30	31			

JUNE

S	M	T	W	T	F	S
				1	2	3
4	5	6	7	8	9	10
11	12	13	14	15	16	17
18	19	20	21	22	23	24
25	26	27	28	29	30	

3
saturday

4
sunday

June

5
monday

6
tuesday

7
wednesday

8
thursday

9
friday

Full Moon ○

10
saturday

11
sunday

June

S	M	T	W	T	F	S
				1	2	3
4	5	6	7	8	9	10
11	12	13	14	15	16	17
18	19	20	21	22	23	24
25	26	27	28	29	30	

July

S	M	T	W	T	F	S
						1
2	3	4	5	6	7	8
9	10	11	12	13	14	15
16	17	18	19	20	21	22
23/30	24/31	25	26	27	28	29

June

12
monday

13
tuesday

14
wednesday

15
thursday

16
friday

June

S	M	T	W	T	F	S
				1	2	3
4	5	6	7	8	9	10
11	12	13	14	15	16	17
18	19	20	21	22	23	24
25	26	27	28	29	30	

July

S	M	T	W	T	F	S
						1
2	3	4	5	6	7	8
9	10	11	12	13	14	15
16	17	18	19	20	21	22
23/30	24/31	25	26	27	28	29

Last Quarter ◑

17
saturday

Father's Day (U.S., Canada, U.K.)

18
sunday

June

19
monday

20
tuesday

21
wednesday
International Day of Yoga Summer Solstice

22
thursday

23
friday
New Moon ●

24
saturday

25
sunday

JUNE

S	M	T	W	T	F	S
				1	2	3
4	5	6	7	8	9	10
11	12	13	14	15	16	17
18	19	20	21	22	23	24
25	26	27	28	29	30	

JULY

S	M	T	W	T	F	S
						1
2	3	4	5	6	7	8
9	10	11	12	13	14	15
16	17	18	19	20	21	22
23/30	24/31	25	26	27	28	29

The beauty of the sky and of all Nature makes a proper altar for the worship of the Infinite.

—Paramahansa Yogananda

Spirit Island, Jasper National Park, Alberta, Canada   Photograph by Michael Wheatley

Love only what is beautiful and pure....See, hear, smell, taste, and touch
only what is good....Will and feel goodness,
and ever seek the sweet nectar of God's presence in meditation.

—Paramahansa Yogananda

Glasswinged butterfly and oleander flowers   Photograph by Tatiana Krylova/500PX

June/July

26
monday

27
tuesday

28
wednesday

29
thursday

30
friday

First Quarter ◐

JUNE

S	M	T	W	T	F	S
				1	2	3
4	5	6	7	8	9	10
11	12	13	14	15	16	17
18	19	20	21	22	23	24
25	26	27	28	29	30	

1
saturday

Canada Day (Canada)

JULY

S	M	T	W	T	F	S
						1
2	3	4	5	6	7	8
9	10	11	12	13	14	15
16	17	18	19	20	21	22
23/30	24/31	25	26	27	28	29

2
sunday

July

3
monday

4
tuesday
Independence Day

5
wednesday

6
thursday

7
friday

8
saturday
Full Moon ◯

9
sunday

JULY

S	M	T	W	T	F	S
						1
2	3	4	5	6	7	8
9	10	11	12	13	14	15
16	17	18	19	20	21	22
23/30	24/31	25	26	27	28	29

AUGUST

S	M	T	W	T	F	S
		1	2	3	4	5
6	7	8	9	10	11	12
13	14	15	16	17	18	19
20	21	22	23	24	25	26
27	28	29	30	31		

Follow the path that leads you to His infinite presence.

—Paramahansa Yogananda

Goat Rocks Wilderness, Washington   Photograph by Kevin McNeal

Sparkling lakes, great mountains, heaving oceans, sky, air, and fire;
man's physical body and his ethereal thoughts —
all are but vibrations of one Cosmic Energy.

—Paramahansa Yogananda

Halemaumau vent of Kilauea volcano, Hawaii   Photograph by G. Brad Lewis

July

10
monday

11
tuesday

12
wednesday

13
thursday

14
friday

JULY

S	M	T	W	T	F	S
						1
2	3	4	5	6	7	8
9	10	11	12	13	14	15
16	17	18	19	20	21	22
23/30	24/31	25	26	27	28	29

15
saturday

AUGUST

S	M	T	W	T	F	S
		1	2	3	4	5
6	7	8	9	10	11	12
13	14	15	16	17	18	19
20	21	22	23	24	25	26
27	28	29	30	31		

16
sunday

Last Quarter ◑

July

17
monday

18
tuesday

19
wednesday

20
thursday

21
friday

22
saturday

23
sunday

New Moon ●

JULY

S	M	T	W	T	F	S
						1
2	3	4	5	6	7	8
9	10	11	12	13	14	15
16	17	18	19	20	21	22
23/30	24/31	25	26	27	28	29

AUGUST

S	M	T	W	T	F	S
		1	2	3	4	5
6	7	8	9	10	11	12
13	14	15	16	17	18	19
20	21	22	23	24	25	26
27	28	29	30	31		

Love is the song of the soul, singing to God.
—Paramahansa Yogananda

Double-collared sunbird atop protea flower, Cape Town, South Africa   Photograph by Kevin Schafer

Problems that have seemed insoluble will unravel their mysteries in the nook of solitary thoughtfulness.

—Paramahansa Yogananda

Rainbow eucalyptus tree grove, Maui, Hawaii   Photograph by Dennis Frates

July

24
monday

25
tuesday
Mahavatar Babaji Commemoration Day

26
wednesday

27
thursday

28
friday

JULY

S	M	T	W	T	F	S
						1
2	3	4	5	6	7	8
9	10	11	12	13	14	15
16	17	18	19	20	21	22
23/30	24/31	25	26	27	28	29

AUGUST

S	M	T	W	T	F	S
		1	2	3	4	5
6	7	8	9	10	11	12
13	14	15	16	17	18	19
20	21	22	23	24	25	26
27	28	29	30	31		

29
saturday

30
sunday
First Quarter ◐

July/August

31
monday

1
tuesday

2
wednesday

3
thursday

4
friday

5
saturday

6
sunday

JULY

S	M	T	W	T	F	S
						1
2	3	4	5	6	7	8
9	10	11	12	13	14	15
16	17	18	19	20	21	22
23/30	24/31	25	26	27	28	29

AUGUST

S	M	T	W	T	F	S
		1	2	3	4	5
6	7	8	9	10	11	12
13	14	15	16	17	18	19
20	21	22	23	24	25	26
27	28	29	30	31		

There is a magnet in your heart that will attract true friends.
That magnet is unselfishness, thinking of others first.

—Paramahansa Yogananda

African penguins, Table Mountain National Park, South Africa Photograph by Stuart Westmorland

Who made the flower a living form, reaching out to the sun? Whence came its fragrance and beauty? How were its petals formed so perfectly, and tinged with lovely colors?...When we see nature's wonders we feel awed by the hidden intelligence behind them.

—Paramahansa Yogananda

Indian paintbrush, Yosemite National Park, California   Photograph by Adam Jones/Dennis Flaherty Photography

August

7
monday

Full Moon ○

8
tuesday

9
wednesday

10
thursday

11
friday

AUGUST

S	M	T	W	T	F	S
		1	2	3	4	5
6	7	8	9	10	11	12
13	14	15	16	17	18	19
20	21	22	23	24	25	26
27	28	29	30	31		

12
saturday

SEPTEMBER

S	M	T	W	T	F	S
					1	2
3	4	5	6	7	8	9
10	11	12	13	14	15	16
17	18	19	20	21	22	23
24	25	26	27	28	29	30

13
sunday

August

14
monday

Last Quarter ◑

15
tuesday

Janmashtami

16
wednesday

17
thursday

18
friday

19
saturday

20
sunday

AUGUST

S	M	T	W	T	F	S
		1	2	3	4	5
6	7	8	9	10	11	12
13	14	15	16	17	18	19
20	21	22	23	24	25	26
27	28	29	30	31		

SEPTEMBER

S	M	T	W	T	F	S
					1	2
3	4	5	6	7	8	9
10	11	12	13	14	15	16
17	18	19	20	21	22	23
24	25	26	27	28	29	30

The whole world is pulsing with the power of God: indescribable, infinite happiness; wave after wave of bliss.

—Paramahansa Yogananda

Breaking waves, Oahu, Hawaii   Photograph by Mark A. Johnson/AGE Fotostock

Whatever path your heart's deep desire tells you to follow is your royal highway in this life, the route you should travel in order to reach the abode of lasting peace and happiness.

—Paramahansa Yogananda

Leslie Gulch, Malheur County, Oregon   Photograph by Dennis Frates

August

21
monday

New Moon ●

22
tuesday

23
wednesday

24
thursday

25
friday

August

S	M	T	W	T	F	S
		1	2	3	4	5
6	7	8	9	10	11	12
13	14	15	16	17	18	19
20	21	22	23	24	25	26
27	28	29	30	31		

26
saturday

September

S	M	T	W	T	F	S
					1	2
3	4	5	6	7	8	9
10	11	12	13	14	15	16
17	18	19	20	21	22	23
24	25	26	27	28	29	30

27
sunday

August/September

28
monday

29
tuesday

First Quarter ◐

30
wednesday

31
thursday

1
friday

2
saturday

3
sunday

AUGUST

S	M	T	W	T	F	S
		1	2	3	4	5
6	7	8	9	10	11	12
13	14	15	16	17	18	19
20	21	22	23	24	25	26
27	28	29	30	31		

SEPTEMBER

S	M	T	W	T	F	S
					1	2
3	4	5	6	7	8	9
10	11	12	13	14	15	16
17	18	19	20	21	22	23
24	25	26	27	28	29	30

If you but *looked* at your soul, the all-perfect reflection of God within you, you would find all your desires satisfied!

—Paramahansa Yogananda

Marsh Lake, John Muir Wilderness, California   Photograph by Adam Jones/Dennis Flaherty Photography

Let God flow through you continuously. Then wherever you go, you will be a magnet.
Even at a distance you can change an enemy.
Just send him your love.

—Paramahansa Yogananda

Red maple, Dryberry Creek, Ontario, Canada   Photograph by Mike Grandmaison

September

4
monday

Labor Day (U.S. and Canada)

5
tuesday

6
wednesday

Full Moon ◯

7
thursday

8
friday

SEPTEMBER

S	M	T	W	T	F	S
					1	2
3	4	5	6	7	8	9
10	11	12	13	14	15	16
17	18	19	20	21	22	23
24	25	26	27	28	29	30

9
saturday

OCTOBER

S	M	T	W	T	F	S
1	2	3	4	5	6	7
8	9	10	11	12	13	14
15	16	17	18	19	20	21
22	23	24	25	26	27	28
29	30	31				

10
sunday

September

11
monday

12
tuesday
Last Quarter ◑

13
wednesday

14
thursday

15
friday

16
saturday

17
sunday

SEPTEMBER

S	M	T	W	T	F	S
					1	2
3	4	5	6	7	8	9
10	11	12	13	14	15	16
17	18	19	20	21	22	23
24	25	26	27	28	29	30

OCTOBER

S	M	T	W	T	F	S
1	2	3	4	5	6	7
8	9	10	11	12	13	14
15	16	17	18	19	20	21
22	23	24	25	26	27	28
29	30	31				

One who gives mental and material help to others
with a heart overflowing with kindness
will find the same coming back to him.

—Paramahansa Yogananda

Red Fox kit, Grand Teton National Park, Wyoming   Photograph by Fi Rust

Like a river, love flows continuously through humble, sincere souls.

—Paramahansa Yogananda

In the Adirondack Mountains, New York Photograph by Christopher Talbot Frank

September

18
monday

19
tuesday

New Moon ●

20
wednesday

Rosh Hashanah

21
thursday

U.N. International Day of Peace

22
friday

Autumnal Equinox

SEPTEMBER

S	M	T	W	T	F	S
					1	2
3	4	5	6	7	8	9
10	11	12	13	14	15	16
17	18	19	20	21	22	23
24	25	26	27	28	29	30

23
saturday

OCTOBER

S	M	T	W	T	F	S
1	2	3	4	5	6	7
8	9	10	11	12	13	14
15	16	17	18	19	20	21
22	23	24	25	26	27	28
29	30	31				

24
sunday

September/October

25
monday

26
tuesday
Lahiri Mahasaya's Mahasamadhi

27
wednesday
First Quarter ◐

28
thursday

29
friday
Yom Kippur

30
saturday
Lahiri Mahasaya's Birthday

1
sunday

September

S	M	T	W	T	F	S
					1	2
3	4	5	6	7	8	9
10	11	12	13	14	15	16
17	18	19	20	21	22	23
24	25	26	27	28	29	30

October

S	M	T	W	T	F	S
1	2	3	4	5	6	7
8	9	10	11	12	13	14
15	16	17	18	19	20	21
22	23	24	25	26	27	28
29	30	31				

O Spirit, in the fragrance of the flowers, in the perfume of minds, show us that Thou art on the altar of nature and in our souls.

—Paramahansa Yogananda

Bluebells and beech trees, Micheldever Woods, Hampshire, England
Photograph by Guy Edwardes/Nature Picture Library

Don't think that the search for God consists only in meditation.
Every good quality that you express in thought and action
yields the hidden nectar of God's presence.

—Paramahansa Yogananda

Costa's Hummingbird, Southwestern U.S.A. Photograph by Anthony Mercieca/AnimalsAnimals

October

2
monday

3
tuesday

4
wednesday

5
thursday

Full Moon ○

6
friday

7
saturday

8
sunday

October

S	M	T	W	T	F	S
1	2	3	4	5	6	7
8	9	10	11	12	13	14
15	16	17	18	19	20	21
22	23	24	25	26	27	28
29	30	31				

November

S	M	T	W	T	F	S
			1	2	3	4
5	6	7	8	9	10	11
12	13	14	15	16	17	18
19	20	21	22	23	24	25
26	27	28	29	30		

October

9
monday

Columbus Day   Thanksgiving Day (Canada)

10
tuesday

11
wednesday

12
thursday

Last Quarter ◑

13
friday

14
saturday

15
sunday

October

S	M	T	W	T	F	S
1	2	3	4	5	6	7
8	9	10	11	12	13	14
15	16	17	18	19	20	21
22	23	24	25	26	27	28
29	30	31				

November

S	M	T	W	T	F	S
			1	2	3	4
5	6	7	8	9	10	11
12	13	14	15	16	17	18
19	20	21	22	23	24	25
26	27	28	29	30		

Stillness is the altar of Spirit. Where motion ceases, Spirit begins to manifest.

—Paramahansa Yogananda

Yosemite National Park, California   Photograph by Loïc Lagarde/500PX

Gain unshakable faith by basing your wisdom and spiritual understanding on your own spiritual experience.

—Paramahansa Yogananda

Balancing Rock, Long Island, Nova Scotia, Canada   Photograph by Thomas & Victoria Kitchin/AGE Fotostock

October

16
monday

17
tuesday

18
wednesday

19
thursday

New Moon ●

20
friday

21
saturday

22
sunday

OCTOBER

S	M	T	W	T	F	S
1	2	3	4	5	6	7
8	9	10	11	12	13	14
15	16	17	18	19	20	21
22	23	24	25	26	27	28
29	30	31				

NOVEMBER

S	M	T	W	T	F	S
			1	2	3	4
5	6	7	8	9	10	11
12	13	14	15	16	17	18
19	20	21	22	23	24	25
26	27	28	29	30		

October

23
monday

24
tuesday

25
wednesday

26
thursday

27
friday

First Quarter ◐

28
saturday

29
sunday

Daylight Saving Time ends (European Union)

October

S	M	T	W	T	F	S
1	2	3	4	5	6	7
8	9	10	11	12	13	14
15	16	17	18	19	20	21
22	23	24	25	26	27	28
29	30	31				

November

S	M	T	W	T	F	S
			1	2	3	4
5	6	7	8	9	10	11
12	13	14	15	16	17	18
19	20	21	22	23	24	25
26	27	28	29	30		

Your

2018 INNER REFLECTIONS ENGAGEMENT CALENDAR

is now available in bookstores.

You may also place your order directly from Self-Realization Fellowship by calling 818-549-5151 Monday – Friday from 9:00 a.m. to 5:00 p.m. Pacific time or order online at:
www.srfbooks.org

If you would like a free copy of Self-Realization Fellowship's complete catalog of books and recordings, please request it by phone or fill out the form below and fax or mail it to:

Self-Realization Fellowship
3880 San Rafael Ave.
Los Angeles, CA 90065-3219 U.S.A.
Fax: 800-801-1952

Name: ______________________________

Address: ______________________________

City: ____________________ State: _____ Zip code: __________

Daytime phone: ____________________ Date: ____________________

The peace of meditation is the language and embracing comfort of God.... When you know God as peace within, then you will realize Him as peace existing in the universal harmony of all things without.

—Paramahansa Yogananda

Ausable River, Sentinel Range Wilderness, Elba, New York Photograph by Paul Rezendes

One who attains the ultimate wisdom realizes that everything is Spirit — in essence, though hidden in manifestation. If you had the perception, you would see God in everything.

—Paramahansa Yogananda

Great Gray Owl, Oregon   Photograph by Art Wolfe

October/November

30
monday

31
tuesday
Halloween (U.S., Canada, U.K.)

1
wednesday

2
thursday

3
friday
Full Moon ○

October

S	M	T	W	T	F	S
1	2	3	4	5	6	7
8	9	10	11	12	13	14
15	16	17	18	19	20	21
22	23	24	25	26	27	28
29	30	31				

November

S	M	T	W	T	F	S
			1	2	3	4
5	6	7	8	9	10	11
12	13	14	15	16	17	18
19	20	21	22	23	24	25
26	27	28	29	30		

4
saturday

5
sunday
Daylight Saving Time ends (U.S. and Canada)

November

6
monday

7
tuesday
General Election Day

8
wednesday

9
thursday

10
friday
Last Quarter ◑

11
saturday
Veterans Day Remembrance Day (Canada)

12
sunday
Remembrance Sunday (U.K.)

NOVEMBER

S	M	T	W	T	F	S
			1	2	3	4
5	6	7	8	9	10	11
12	13	14	15	16	17	18
19	20	21	22	23	24	25
26	27	28	29	30		

DECEMBER

S	M	T	W	T	F	S
					1	2
3	4	5	6	7	8	9
10	11	12	13	14	15	16
17	18	19	20	21	22	23
24/31	25	26	27	28	29	30

Love is the ocean of eternal unity, where the meandering rivers of all little lives
are to merge into the resplendent vastness
of blissful, immortal Spirit.

—Paramahansa Yogananda

Headwaters of the Nass River, British Columbia, Canada Photograph by Carr Clifton

Keep life simple and enjoy what God has provided.
—Paramahansa Yogananda

Porcupine, Pine County, Minnesota   Photograph by Cathy & Gordon Illg

November

13
monday

14
tuesday

15
wednesday

16
thursday

17
friday

NOVEMBER

S	M	T	W	T	F	S
			1	2	3	4
5	6	7	8	9	10	11
12	13	14	15	16	17	18
19	20	21	22	23	24	25
26	27	28	29	30		

New Moon ●

18
saturday

DECEMBER

S	M	T	W	T	F	S
					1	2
3	4	5	6	7	8	9
10	11	12	13	14	15	16
17	18	19	20	21	22	23
24/31	25	26	27	28	29	30

19
sunday

November

20
monday

21
tuesday

22
wednesday

23
thursday

Thanksgiving Day

24
friday

25
saturday

26
sunday

First Quarter ◐

NOVEMBER

S	M	T	W	T	F	S
			1	2	3	4
5	6	7	8	9	10	11
12	13	14	15	16	17	18
19	20	21	22	23	24	25
26	27	28	29	30		

DECEMBER

S	M	T	W	T	F	S
					1	2
3	4	5	6	7	8	9
10	11	12	13	14	15	16
17	18	19	20	21	22	23
24/31	25	26	27	28	29	30

Every day should be a day of thanksgiving for the gifts of life:
sunshine, water, and the luscious fruits and greens
that are indirect gifts of the Great Giver.

—Paramahansa Yogananda

Lake Bohinj, Triglav National Park, Slovenia   Photograph by Guy Edwardes

All the miracles of life that we take for granted
are proof of the existence of an omnipresent divine Intelligence
behind the processes of nature.

—Paramahansa Yogananda

Loch Dunmore, Pitlochry, Tayside, Scotland   Photograph by Tom Mackie

November/December

27
monday

28
tuesday

29
wednesday

30
thursday

1
friday

November

S	M	T	W	T	F	S
			1	2	3	4
5	6	7	8	9	10	11
12	13	14	15	16	17	18
19	20	21	22	23	24	25
26	27	28	29	30		

December

S	M	T	W	T	F	S
					1	2
3	4	5	6	7	8	9
10	11	12	13	14	15	16
17	18	19	20	21	22	23
24/31	25	26	27	28	29	30

2
saturday

Full Moon ○

3
sunday

December

4
monday

5
tuesday

6
wednesday

7
thursday

8
friday

9
saturday

Last Quarter ◑

10
sunday

December

S	M	T	W	T	F	S
					1	2
3	4	5	6	7	8	9
10	11	12	13	14	15	16
17	18	19	20	21	22	23
24/31	25	26	27	28	29	30

January 2018

S	M	T	W	T	F	S
	1	2	3	4	5	6
7	8	9	10	11	12	13
14	15	16	17	18	19	20
21	22	23	24	25	26	27
28	29	30	31			

When you pray with deep sincerity, all restless thoughts fall away, all sensory distractions vanish, and in that stillness you find Him coming to you. Then you will realize how wonderful life is.

—Paramahansa Yogananda

Tully River, Royalston, Massachusetts Photograph by Paul Rezendes

If in deep meditation you penetrate the darkness behind closed eyes, you behold the Light from which all creation emerges.

—Paramahansa Yogananda

Glacial lagoon with aurora, Jökulsárlón, Iceland Photograph by Josh Anon

December

11
monday

12
tuesday
Hanukkah

13
wednesday

14
thursday

15
friday

16
saturday

17
sunday
New Moon ●

December

S	M	T	W	T	F	S
					1	2
3	4	5	6	7	8	9
10	11	12	13	14	15	16
17	18	19	20	21	22	23
24/31	25	26	27	28	29	30

January 2018

S	M	T	W	T	F	S
	1	2	3	4	5	6
7	8	9	10	11	12	13
14	15	16	17	18	19	20
21	22	23	24	25	26	27
28	29	30	31			

December

18
monday

19
tuesday

20
wednesday

21
thursday

Winter Solstice

22
friday

23
saturday

24
sunday

DECEMBER

S	M	T	W	T	F	S
					1	2
3	4	5	6	7	8	9
10	11	12	13	14	15	16
17	18	19	20	21	22	23
24/31	25	26	27	28	29	30

JANUARY 2018

S	M	T	W	T	F	S
	1	2	3	4	5	6
7	8	9	10	11	12	13
14	15	16	17	18	19	20
21	22	23	24	25	26	27
28	29	30	31			

Today I will open the door of my calmness
and let the footsteps of silence enter the temple of all my activities.

—Paramahansa Yogananda

Junction Creek, Greater Sudbury, Ontario, Canada   Photograph by Don Johnston

Each year at Christmastime there are stronger than usual vibrations of Christ-love and joy
that emanate to earth from the heavenly realms.
The ether becomes filled with the Infinite Light
that shone on earth when Jesus was born.

—Paramahansa Yogananda

Sunrise, Monte Falterona, Italy   Photograph by Roberto Melotti/500PX

December

25
monday

Christmas

26
tuesday

Boxing Day (Canada, U.K., Australia, N.Z.)   First Quarter ◐

27
wednesday

28
thursday

29
friday

DECEMBER

S	M	T	W	T	F	S
					1	2
3	4	5	6	7	8	9
10	11	12	13	14	15	16
17	18	19	20	21	22	23
24/31	25	26	27	28	29	30

JANUARY 2018

S	M	T	W	T	F	S
	1	2	3	4	5	6
7	8	9	10	11	12	13
14	15	16	17	18	19	20
21	22	23	24	25	26	27
28	29	30	31			

30
saturday

31
sunday

NOTES

ACKNOWLEDGMENTS

We wish to express our sincere appreciation to the following photographers and agencies who contributed to this year's *Inner Reflections* engagement calendar. Following a contributor's name, in parentheses, is the month and a day of the week, or other description, where each photo appears.

500PX (1/30, 2/13, 3/27, 5/22, 6/26, 10/9, 12/25)

AGE Fotostock (2/27, 6/12, 8/14, 10/16)

AKM Images (5/8, 5/29)

AnimalsAnimals (4/24, 5/1, 10/2)

Josh Anon (12/11)

Kul Bhatia/AGE Fotostock (6/12)

Carr Clifton (11/6)

Claudio Contreras (1/16)

Guy Edwardes (11/20)

Guy Edwardes/Nature Picture Library (9/25)

Geoff du Feu/AnimalsAnimals (4/24)

First Light (4/17)

Adam Jones/Dennis Flaherty Photography (8/7, 8/28)

Christopher Talbot Frank (9/18)

Dennis Frates (1/23, 7/24, 8/21)

Bernard Friel (1/2)

Mike Grandmaison (9/4)

Per-Andre Hoffmann/AGE Fotostock (2/27)

George H. H. Huey (3/13)

Cathy & Gordon Illg (11/13)

A. Jeffry/500PX (3/27)

Mark A. Johnson/AGE Fotostock (8/14)

Don Johnston (12/18)

Cindy Kassab/AKM Images (5/8)

Stephen Kirkpatrick (1/9)

Thomas & Victoria Kitchin/AGE Fotostock (10/16)

Thomas Kraft (4/10)

Tatiana Krylova/500PX (6/26)

Loïc Lagarde/500PX (10/9)

G. Brad Lewis (7/10)

Tom Mackie (12/26/16, 11/27)

Roine Magnusson/First Light (4/17)

Kathy Mahan (4/3, 5/15)

Mauro Malone/500PX (5/22)

Luiz Claudio Marigo/AnimalsAnimals (5/1)

Kevin McNeal (7/3)

Roberto Melotti/500PX (12/25)

Anthony Mercieca/AnimalsAnimals (10/2)

Minden Pictures (3/6)

Juliana Nan/500PX (2/13)

Nature Picture Library (9/25)

Jim Nelson/500PX (1/30)

Marion Owen (2/6)

Don Paulson (Cover, 6/5)

Paul Rezendes (10/23, 12/4)

Fi Rust (9/11)

George Sanker/AKM Images (5/29)

Kevin Schafer (7/17)

Kevin Schafer/Minden Pictures (3/6)

Dave Welling (3/20)

Stuart Westmorland (7/31)

Michael Wheatley (2/20, 6/19)

Art Wolfe (10/30)

About Paramahansa Yogananda

Paramahansa Yogananda
1893-1952

All the quotes featured in *Inner Reflections* have been selected from the writings of Paramahansa Yogananda, one of the preeminent spiritual teachers of the 20th century. Yogananda came to the United States in 1920 as India's delegate to an international congress of religious leaders convening in Boston. He remained in the West for the better part of the next thirty-two years, conducting classes in cities across America, counseling, and creating a monumental body of written work.

Paramahansa Yogananda's life story, *Autobiography of a Yogi*, is considered a modern spiritual classic. It was selected one of "The Top 100 Spiritual Books of the Twentieth Century" in a survey conducted by HarperCollins. A perennial best seller since it was first published in 1946, *Autobiography of a Yogi* has been translated into more than forty languages and is widely used in college and university courses.

An award-winning documentary about Paramahansa Yogananda's life and work, *Awake: The Life of Yogananda*, was released in October, 2014.

For more information about SRF publications and the teachings of Paramahansa Yogananda, please visit our website:

www.yogananda-srf.org

Self-Realization Fellowship

FOUNDED 1920 BY PARAMAHANSA YOGANANDA

SELF-REALIZATION FELLOWSHIP, the international nonprofit society founded by Paramahansa Yogananda, is dedicated to carrying on his spiritual and humanitarian work — fostering a spirit of greater harmony and understanding among those of all nations and faiths, and introducing truth-seekers around the world to his universal teachings on the ancient science of Yoga.

A SELECTION OF BOOKS BY PARAMAHANSA YOGANANDA

Available at bookstores or from our website:
www.srfbooks.org

Autobiography of a Yogi
(Ebook editions also available from Amazon Kindle and Apple iTunes)

Autobiography of a Yogi *(Audiobook, read by Sir Ben Kingsley)*

The Science of Religion

The Law of Success

How You Can Talk With God

Metaphysical Meditations

Where There Is Light: *Insight and Inspiration for Meeting Life's Challenges*

The Yoga of Jesus: *Understanding the Hidden Teachings of the Gospels*

The Yoga of the Bhagavad Gita: *An Introduction to India's Universal Science of God-Realization*

The Collected Talks and Essays
Volume I: Man's Eternal Quest
Volume II: The Divine Romance
Volume III: Journey to Self-realization

DVD VIDEO

Awake: The Life of Yogananda
A film by CounterPoint Films

SELF-REALIZATION FELLOWSHIP LESSONS

The scientific techniques of meditation taught by Paramahansa Yogananda, including *Kriya Yoga* — as well as his guidance on all aspects of balanced spiritual living — are taught in the *Self-Realization Fellowship Lessons*. For further information, we welcome you to request the free booklet *Undreamed-of Possibilities*.

SELF-REALIZATION FELLOWSHIP

3880 San Rafael Avenue • Los Angeles, CA 90065-3219

TEL (323) 225-2471 • FAX (323) 225-5088

www.yogananda-srf.org

2016

January

s	m	t	w	t	f	s
					1	2
3	4	5	6	7	8	9
10	11	12	13	14	15	16
17	18	19	20	21	22	23
24/31	25	26	27	28	29	30

February

s	m	t	w	t	f	s
	1	2	3	4	5	6
7	8	9	10	11	12	13
14	15	16	17	18	19	20
21	22	23	24	25	26	27
28	29					

March

s	m	t	w	t	f	s
		1	2	3	4	5
6	7	8	9	10	11	12
13	14	15	16	17	18	19
20	21	22	23	24	25	26
27	28	29	30	31		

April

s	m	t	w	t	f	s
					1	2
3	4	5	6	7	8	9
10	11	12	13	14	15	16
17	18	19	20	21	22	23
24	25	26	27	28	29	30

May

s	m	t	w	t	f	s
1	2	3	4	5	6	7
8	9	10	11	12	13	14
15	16	17	18	19	20	21
22	23	24	25	26	27	28
29	30	31				

June

s	m	t	w	t	f	s
			1	2	3	4
5	6	7	8	9	10	11
12	13	14	15	16	17	18
19	20	21	22	23	24	25
26	27	28	29	30		

July

s	m	t	w	t	f	s
					1	2
3	4	5	6	7	8	9
10	11	12	13	14	15	16
17	18	19	20	21	22	23
24/31	25	26	27	28	29	30

August

s	m	t	w	t	f	s
	1	2	3	4	5	6
7	8	9	10	11	12	13
14	15	16	17	18	19	20
21	22	23	24	25	26	27
28	29	30	31			

September

s	m	t	w	t	f	s
				1	2	3
4	5	6	7	8	9	10
11	12	13	14	15	16	17
18	19	20	21	22	23	24
25	26	27	28	29	30	

October

s	m	t	w	t	f	s
						1
2	3	4	5	6	7	8
9	10	11	12	13	14	15
16	17	18	19	20	21	22
23/30	24/31	25	26	27	28	29

November

s	m	t	w	t	f	s
		1	2	3	4	5
6	7	8	9	10	11	12
13	14	15	16	17	18	19
20	21	22	23	24	25	26
27	28	29	30			

December

s	m	t	w	t	f	s
				1	2	3
4	5	6	7	8	9	10
11	12	13	14	15	16	17
18	19	20	21	22	23	24
25	26	27	28	29	30	31

2018

January

s	m	t	w	t	f	s
	1	2	3	4	5	6
7	8	9	10	11	12	13
14	15	16	17	18	19	20
21	22	23	24	25	26	27
28	29	30	31			

February

s	m	t	w	t	f	s
				1	2	3
4	5	6	7	8	9	10
11	12	13	14	15	16	17
18	19	20	21	22	23	24
25	26	27	28			

March

s	m	t	w	t	f	s
				1	2	3
4	5	6	7	8	9	10
11	12	13	14	15	16	17
18	19	20	21	22	23	24
25	26	27	28	29	30	31

April

s	m	t	w	t	f	s
1	2	3	4	5	6	7
8	9	10	11	12	13	14
15	16	17	18	19	20	21
22	23	24	25	26	27	28
29	30					

May

s	m	t	w	t	f	s
		1	2	3	4	5
6	7	8	9	10	11	12
13	14	15	16	17	18	19
20	21	22	23	24	25	26
27	28	29	30	31		

June

s	m	t	w	t	f	s
					1	2
3	4	5	6	7	8	9
10	11	12	13	14	15	16
17	18	19	20	21	22	23
24	25	26	27	28	29	30

July

s	m	t	w	t	f	s
1	2	3	4	5	6	7
8	9	10	11	12	13	14
15	16	17	18	19	20	21
22	23	24	25	26	27	28
29	30	31				

August

s	m	t	w	t	f	s
			1	2	3	4
5	6	7	8	9	10	11
12	13	14	15	16	17	18
19	20	21	22	23	24	25
26	27	28	29	30	31	

September

s	m	t	w	t	f	s
						1
2	3	4	5	6	7	8
9	10	11	12	13	14	15
16	17	18	19	20	21	22
23/30	24	25	26	27	28	29

October

s	m	t	w	t	f	s
	1	2	3	4	5	6
7	8	9	10	11	12	13
14	15	16	17	18	19	20
21	22	23	24	25	26	27
28	29	30	31			

November

s	m	t	w	t	f	s
				1	2	3
4	5	6	7	8	9	10
11	12	13	14	15	16	17
18	19	20	21	22	23	24
25	26	27	28	29	30	

December

s	m	t	w	t	f	s
						1
2	3	4	5	6	7	8
9	10	11	12	13	14	15
16	17	18	19	20	21	22
23/30	24/31	25	26	27	28	29

2017

January

s	m	t	w	t	f	s
1	2	3	4	5	6	7
8	9	10	11	12	13	14
15	16	17	18	19	20	21
22	23	24	25	26	27	28
29	30	31				

February

s	m	t	w	t	f	s
			1	2	3	4
5	6	7	8	9	10	11
12	13	14	15	16	17	18
19	20	21	22	23	24	25
26	27	28				

March

s	m	t	w	t	f	s
			1	2	3	4
5	6	7	8	9	10	11
12	13	14	15	16	17	18
19	20	21	22	23	24	25
26	27	28	29	30	31	

April

s	m	t	w	t	f	s
						1
2	3	4	5	6	7	8
9	10	11	12	13	14	15
16	17	18	19	20	21	22
23/30	24	25	26	27	28	29

May

s	m	t	w	t	f	s
	1	2	3	4	5	6
7	8	9	10	11	12	13
14	15	16	17	18	19	20
21	22	23	24	25	26	27
28	29	30	31			

June

s	m	t	w	t	f	s
				1	2	3
4	5	6	7	8	9	10
11	12	13	14	15	16	17
18	19	20	21	22	23	24
25	26	27	28	29	30	

July

s	m	t	w	t	f	s
						1
2	3	4	5	6	7	8
9	10	11	12	13	14	15
16	17	18	19	20	21	22
23/30	24/31	25	26	27	28	29

August

s	m	t	w	t	f	s
		1	2	3	4	5
6	7	8	9	10	11	12
13	14	15	16	17	18	19
20	21	22	23	24	25	26
27	28	29	30	31		

September

s	m	t	w	t	f	s
					1	2
3	4	5	6	7	8	9
10	11	12	13	14	15	16
17	18	19	20	21	22	23
24	25	26	27	28	29	30

October

s	m	t	w	t	f	s
1	2	3	4	5	6	7
8	9	10	11	12	13	14
15	16	17	18	19	20	21
22	23	24	25	26	27	28
29	30	31				

November

s	m	t	w	t	f	s
			1	2	3	4
5	6	7	8	9	10	11
12	13	14	15	16	17	18
19	20	21	22	23	24	25
26	27	28	29	30		

December

s	m	t	w	t	f	s
					1	2
3	4	5	6	7	8	9
10	11	12	13	14	15	16
17	18	19	20	21	22	23
24/31	25	26	27	28	29	30

JANUARY

Sunday	Monday	Tuesday	Wednesday	Thursday	Friday	Saturday
1	2	3	4	5	6	7
8	9	10	11	12	13	14
15	16	17	18	19	20	21
22	23	24	25	26	27	28
29	30	31				

Jan. 1 New Year's Day
Jan. 2 New Year's Day (Observed)
Jan. 5 Paramahansa Yogananda's Birthday
Jan. 16 Martin Luther King, Jr.'s Birthday (Observed)
Jan. 26 Australia Day (Australia)

FEBRUARY

Sunday	Monday	Tuesday	Wednesday	Thursday	Friday	Saturday
			1	2	3	4
5	6	7	8	9	10	11
12	13	14	15	16	17	18
19	20	21	22	23	24	25
26	27	28				

Feb. 14 St. Valentine's Day
Feb. 20 Presidents' Day

March

Sunday	Monday	Tuesday	Wednesday	Thursday	Friday	Saturday
			1	2	3	4
5	6	7	8	9	10	11
12	13	14	15	16	17	18
19	20	21	22	23	24	25
26	27	28	29	30	31	

March 7 Paramahansa Yogananda's Mahasamadhi
March 9 Sri Yukteswar's Mahasamadhi
March 12 Daylight Saving Time begins (U.S. and Canada)
March 17 St. Patrick's Day
March 20 Vernal Equinox
March 26 Daylight Savings Time begins (European Union)

April

Sunday	Monday	Tuesday	Wednesday	Thursday	Friday	Saturday
						1
2	3	4	5	6	7	8
9	10	11	12	13	14	15
16	17	18	19	20	21	22
23	24	25	26	27	28	29
30						

April 10 Passover begins
April 14 Good Friday
April 16 Easter Sunday
April 17 Easter Monday (All except U.S. and Scotland)
April 22 Earth Day

May

Sunday	Monday	Tuesday	Wednesday	Thursday	Friday	Saturday
	1	2	3	4	5	6
7	8	9	10	11	12	13
14	15	16	17	18	19	20
21	22	23	24	25	26	27
28	29	30	31			

May 4 National Day of Prayer
May 10 Sri Yukteswar's Birthday
May 14 Mother's Day (U.S., Canada, Australia, N.Z.)
May 22 Victoria Day (Canada)
May 29 Memorial Day

June

Sunday	Monday	Tuesday	Wednesday	Thursday	Friday	Saturday
				1	2	3
4	5	6	7	8	9	10
11	12	13	14	15	16	17
18	19	20	21	22	23	24
25	26	27	28	29	30	

June 18 Father's Day (U.S., Canada, U.K.)

June 21 Summer Solstice
International Day of Yoga

July

Sunday	Monday	Tuesday	Wednesday	Thursday	Friday	Saturday
						1
2	3	4	5	6	7	8
9	10	11	12	13	14	15
16	17	18	19	20	21	22
23	24	25	26	27	28	29
30	31					

July 1 Canada Day (Canada)
July 4 Independence Day
July 25 Mahavatar Babaji Commemoration Day

AUGUST

Sunday	Monday	Tuesday	Wednesday	Thursday	Friday	Saturday
		1	2	3	4	5
6	7	8	9	10	11	12
13	14	15	16	17	18	19
20	21	22	23	24	25	26
27	28	29	30	31		

Aug. 15 Janmashtami

SEPTEMBER

Sunday	Monday	Tuesday	Wednesday	Thursday	Friday	Saturday
					1	2
3	4	5	6	7	8	9
10	11	12	13	14	15	16
17	18	19	20	21	22	23
24	25	26	27	28	29	30

Sept. 4 Labor Day (U.S. and Canada)
Sept 20 Rosh Hashanah
Sept. 21 U.N. International Day of Peace
Sept. 22 Autumnal Equinox
Sept. 26 Lahiri Mahasaya's Mahasamadhi
Sept 29 Yom Kippur
Sept. 30 Lahiri Mahasaya's Birthday

October

Sunday	Monday	Tuesday	Wednesday	Thursday	Friday	Saturday
1	2	3	4	5	6	7
8	9	10	11	12	13	14
15	16	17	18	19	20	21
22	23	24	25	26	27	28
29	30	31				

Oct. 9 Columbus Day
Thanksgiving Day (Canada)

Oct. 29 Daylight Saving Time ends (European Union)

Oct. 31 Halloween (U.S., Canada, U.K.)

November

Sunday	Monday	Tuesday	Wednesday	Thursday	Friday	Saturday
			1	2	3	4
5	6	7	8	9	10	11
12	13	14	15	16	17	18
19	20	21	22	23	24	25
26	27	28	29	30		

Nov. 5 Daylight Saving Time ends (U.S. and Canada)

Nov. 7 General Election Day

Nov. 11 Veterans Day
Remembrance Day (Canada)

Nov. 12 Remembrance Sunday (U.K.)

Nov. 23 Thanksgiving Day

December

Sunday	Monday	Tuesday	Wednesday	Thursday	Friday	Saturday
					1	2
3	4	5	6	7	8	9
10	11	12	13	14	15	16
17	18	19	20	21	22	23
24	25	26	27	28	29	30
31						

Dec. 12 Hanukkah
Dec. 21 Winter Solstice
Dec. 25 Christmas
Dec. 26 Boxing Day (Canada, U.K., Australia, N.Z.)

NOTES